GALLOPADE!, The World's Largest Publishing Company Presents . . .

INDIANA INDIANS:

A Kid's Look at Our State's Chiefs, Tribes, Reservations, Powwows, Lore & More From the Past & the Present

By Carole Marsh

©1998 Carole Marsh/Gallopade, 200 Northlake Dr., Peachtree City, GA 30269/1-800-536-2GET/Page 1

977.2
MAR
9-00
1177950

More by Carole Marsh

The American Indian Dictionary for Kids! Book: This edition is not state-specific, but general in nature. Available in paperback, hardcover & on computer diskette. And, **The American Indian Dictionary for Kids! Book:** Available in editions for each U. S. state & Canada.

The American Indian Dictionary for Kids! CD-ROM: Features North American Indian tribes, history, reservations, art, family life, women & children, & much more + interactive activities, math, pop quiz, paint programs & more. Packaged in a tepee! Excellent research & report resource for students 7-14. Also available: Teacher's Guide & Reproducible Activities.

Death Valley! & The Secret of Scotty's Castle: An interactive multimedia program on disk for Macintosh or Windows. Features extensive information on Death Valley plus an original children's mystery set at Scotty's Castle.

The *(Phantastic!)* **Petrified Forest & the** *(Phenomenal!)* **Painted Desert:** An interactive multimedia program filled with history, science, art activities & more. For Macintosh or Windows.

Grand Canyon!: A Top-to-Bottom Look at the Mother-of-All-Holes-in-the-Ground!: An interactive multimedia program including information about this area's past & present. For Macintosh or Windows.

Those Whose Names Were Terrible!: Students discover the difference between the myths, legends, rumors & outright errors about Native Americans . . . and the reality!

Christopher Columbus Comes to Indiana!: Editions available for each state. Covers the impact of the explorer's discovery & what it meant to the "Indians" already living in America.

©1998 Carole Marsh/Gallopade, 200 Northlake Dr., Peachtree City, GA 30269/1-800-536-2GET/Page 2

Table of Contents

Howl 4

Indiana Indian Dictionary A-Z 5

Writing Activity 31

Bibliography 32

Think Tank 33

Glossary 34

Pop Quiz 35

Answers 36

How!

Hello!

I hope you are as interested in North America's wonderful Indian heritage as I am!

Like most kids, I grew up thinking of Indians as the other half of Cowboys. Today, of course, we are getting a much clearer & more accurate picture of what the first peoples on our land were all about. These "facts" are much more fascinating than anything Hollywood can make up. And you probably won't find much of this information in your history textbook!

I am 1/16 Cherokee. This is something I am very proud of & happy about. My grandmother was 1/4 Cherokee. She had tan skin, long gray hair & a very Indian look – especially if I did something bad! Her maiden name was Carrie Corn. Of course, when she got married, she took her husband's name, so it was many years before I learned to appreciate the significance of my native heritage.

Today, I'm trying to make up for lost time by exploring my roots as deeply as I can. One of the most interesting things I've learned is how fascinating all of the Indian tribes are – in the past, the present & future!

As you read about "your" Indians, remember that all native peoples were part of an ever-changing network of time, ideas, power & luck — good & bad. This is certainly a history that is not "dead," but continues to change – often right outside our own back doors! – all the time.

Carole Marsh, *She-Who-Writes*
PS: Many references show different spellings for the same word. I have tried to select the most common spelling for the time period described. I would not want to be in an Indian spelling bee!

Aborigine: A member of the earliest known population of a region.

Adze: An Indian wood-working tool used to cut, scrape or gouge. Blades were made of stone, shell, bone or copper. Often used to hollow dugout canoes.

Agriculture: Early Indianans slowly learned to farm. Corn & squash were the staple crops. They used tools like stone axes to clear trees & bowls to grind corn.

American Indian Studies Research Institute: Indiana University, Bloomington.

American Society for Ethnohistory: Goshen; anthropologists, historians, geographers & others promote the study of world societies & cultures & cultural change & history.

Angel Mounds State Historic Site: Evansville. Archaeologists estimate that these 11 mounds were the center of a village where 3,000 early Indianans once lived. This was a large palisaded settlement on the Ohio River occupied from A. D. 1200 to 1450. Inhabitants were of the Mississippian culture. One mound is 44 feet high; another 4 acres in area. Built in the form of truncated pyramids. Not used for burials, but as the base of important buildings. The mile-long stockade was built in wattle & daub & made of 4,500 vertical logs. Here you can see replicas of an Indian dwelling, meetinghouse & temple.

Arts & Crafts: Early Indiana Indians made beautifully decorated pottery, finely carved stone figures of animals & human beings & sparkling jewelry.

Baskets: Made from roots, grasses, barks & other natural materials. Some were woven, others coiled. Basketwork was also used for fences, fish nets, houses, mats, shields, cradles & other items.

Battle of Fallen Timbers: Where the Miami & other tribes were defeated by the Americans. After this, the British encouraged Great Lakes Indians to attack American settlements in the Northwest Territory.

Battle of Tippecanoe: November, 1811; fought just north of Lafayette. Indians charged the American camp with so much courage that the troops at first fell back. But the American's firepower cut down the attackers. This defeat ended Shawnee Chief Tecumseh's dream to unite all Indian tribes to resist the expansion of whites into their lands.

Beads: Made of wood, shells, claws, minerals, seeds — you name it! Worn by Indians & traded with settlers for glass beads.

Before the White Man: About 100,000 people lived in the Great Lakes region when European explorers 1st came to America's east coast.

Blankets: Used for door covers, partitions, bags, to dry food on, carry babies & many other purposes. Woven from animal hair, skins, bark or feathers.

Bone: Animal bones were used by Indians to make buttons, whistles & other items.

"Bury the Hatchet!": Expression that came into being when Chief Pontiac ended his war against the British at Fort Ouiatenon. He flung his tomahawk to the ground, indicating his willingness to stop fighting & start negotiating peace.

Calendar: Time was kept with notched sticks, knotted strings or a picture record. Days were divided into sunrise, noon, sunset & midnight. A full day was called a "night." Months were called "moons." Most Indians called a year a "winter."

Calumet: Also called "peace pipe" or "war pipe." Refers to the stem of the pipe, which is decorated with feathers or carved to signal the tribe's intentions. Believed to have great power.

Chechawkose: Potawatomi chief who lived on the Tippecanoe River.

Chief: Leader of a tribe. Different titles meant different things. Some members were made chief because they owned deeds to land. Chieftainship was often inherited, usually from the mother!

Civil Rights Commission on Indian Affairs: Located in Indianapolis.

Clan: A tribal unit. Members are descended from the same ancestor.

"Contact Period:" What historians call the era in the 1500s when Native Americans 1st met Europeans. This meeting changed the lifestyle of the Indian more than anyone could ever have anticipated!

Council Oak: Tree in Highland Cemetery at South Bend that is believed to be the site of a meeting between La Salle & tribal chiefs more than 300 years ago!

Cultural Center Minnetrista: Muncie; headquarters for Great Lakes Native American Studies.

Dance: There were Indian dances for every occasion: war, peace, hunting, rain or good harvests. Drums, rattles & flutes of bone or reed made music. Chants or songs were often sung while dancing. Many of the dance steps were quite difficult & required a lot of practice.

Delaware: Indians also called the Lenni Lenape; came to Indiana to flee the domination of the Iroquois. Most important confederacy of the Algonquian. The English called them Delawares from their river. The French called them loups or "wolves."

Descendants: The 1st Indianans were descendants of primitive hunters who crossed the Bering Strait from Asia to what is now Alaska. At that time, glacial ice still covered most of North America. These people were the true discovers of the "New World!"

Did You Know You Could Go?: To these Indiana Indian museums: Indiana University Museum, Bloomington, 100,000 artifacts & 15,000 photographs!: William Hammond Mathers Museum, Bloomington, 30,000 artifacts & 8,000 photos; Angel Mounds Library, Evansville; Potawatomi Museum, Fremont, 5,000 prehistoric & historic items; Children's Museum of Indianapolis, 2,000 Indian artifacts; Museum of Indian Heritage, Indianapolis, Indian archaeology collection; Northern Indiana Historical Society Museum, South Bend, Mound Builders exhibit.

Disease: Indians had no immunity to the diseases that white explorers, colonists & settlers brought to their lands. These diseases included smallpox, measles, tuberculosis & others, which ravaged the tribes in great epidemics that killed many, sometimes all, members of a tribe.

Eagle: Used in many Indian ceremonies. Feathers were put on war bonnets, rattles, shields, pipes, baskets & prayer sticks. You could tell an Indian's rank in the tribe & the deeds he had done by the kind of feathers he wore & how he wore them.

Early Artisans: Ancient Great Lakes artisans learned how to hammer copper into axheads & spear points. They often found copper lying in chunks on the ground. By trial & error, they learned how to remove raw copper from inside certain rocks.

Earring: "Pierced" ears are nothing new! Boy & girl Indians had their ears "bored" by medicine men; parents or relatives had to pay for the special ceremony. The more earrings worn, the greater the honor. Some earrings were 1 foot long!

Eel River: Site of Little Turtle's Village; what is today Fort Wayne.

Eel River Indians: Part of the Miami who once lived in Boone County, Indiana.

Eiteljorg Museum of American Indians & Western Art: Indianapolis; paintings, sculpture & more from the 19th century to the present, including the collection of the Museum of Indian Heritage.

English: The first English contacts with Indians were friendly. But in 1605, things changed: many white men began to take advantage of the Indians, killing many & running others off their land. In the late 1600s & late 1790s, colleges were established to help educate the Indian.

Farmers: Around 1,000 B. C., the people of Indiana developed farming techniques & so depended less on hunting. This let them establish permanent villages & spend time on crafts.

First on the Land: Archaeologists believe early human beings pushed in to the Great Lakes region sometime after the last great ice sheet retreated northwest, about 10,000 years ago. The 1st Indianans were wandering bands of hunters. Around 7000 B. C., the climate warmed & pine & birch forests sprang up. The early people began to make tools, jewelry & other objects from local materials.

Fort Miami: One of the Indiana forts which fell to the Indians during the French & Indian War.

French & Indian War: Broke out in 1745 over boundary lines between New France & the British colonies. The British defeated the French & their Indian allies. A peace treaty in 1763 ended the war, when Canada & most French possessions east of the Mississippi River were given to the English.

Friends on Indian Affairs: Richmond; missionary project of the Quakers to Indian Centers.

Fur Trade: Begun when the Europeans came eager to grow rich from the pelts of animals. Trading had a powerful impact on the Indian. To get the newcomers' goods, Indians worked as trappers for the French. A flintlock gun cost 12 beaver pelts. But the ultimate cost was much more expensive — the loss of the Indian's way of life. Many Indians abandoned their traditional farming for trapping & came to depend on the Europeans for the necessities of life.

Fort Wayne: Miami Indians once had a large village near the confluence of the Wabash, St. Marys & St. Joseph Rivers. The Indians attracted the French, who wanted them to get pelts for them.

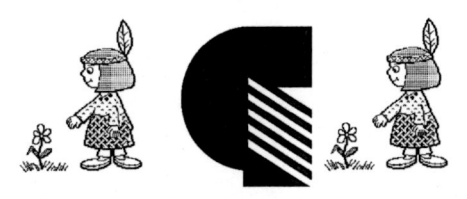

Games: Adults were the ones who played ball & other games of chance or skill. Indian children played by spinning tops, fighting fake battles, target-shooting, walking on stilts, playing hide & seek or seeing who could hold their breath the longest!

General "Mad" Anthony Wayne: Fought the Miami & other tribes in 1794 at the Battle of Fallen Timbers in present-day Ohio. After the battle, he marched into Indiana & built Fort Wayne.

Gens: Group of related members from different tribes.

Godfroy, Francis: Half French & half Indian. Became a Miami chief & led the tribe in its last war party. Opened a trading post near the town of Peru & became rich.

Golden Garbage!: Archaeologists have uncovered ancient garbage heaps made of animal bones & big piles of clam shells in Indiana. This trash full of treasures has helped them understand the early native inhabitants of our state better.

Go To These Exciting Indiana Indian Events!: Turning Leaves Festival, Thorntown, September; Tecumseh Lodge Annual Powwow, Tipton, Labor Day Weekend; Summer Powwow, Harford City, June; Kee-Boon-Mein-Kaa Powwow, South Bend, Labor Day Weekend; AICI Annual Traditional Powwow, Lebanon, August; Honoring All Veterans Powwow, Lebanon, August; Annual Springs Traditional Powwow, Indianapolis, April.

Gorgets: Ornaments hung around the neck or from ears for beauty. Significance, if any, is unknown.

Gourds: The hollowed-out shell of the dried fruit of a gourd plant. Indians raised many species used for food, spoons, bowls, masks, rattles & storage.

Hair: Indians used hair as a textile. Bison, mountain sheep, elk, moose, deer, dog, rabbit, beaver & human hair were used to weave cloth, make wigs, or stuff pillows, balls, dolls or drumsticks.

Hatchet: A small, short-handled ax. Primarily used as a tool, not as a weapon. When settlers moved in, stone hatchets were replaced with iron.

Hopewell Culture: Early people who lived in the Ohio Valley from about 100 B. C. to A. D. 500. Anthropologists believe they had a layered society with a defined organization & code of conduct. Because of this, they could work together to build great earthworks called mounds. They also had an extensive trade network from the Midwest to the eastern U. S. seacoast.

Horn & Hooves: Indians used animal horn to make spoons & dishes. Hooves were made into rattles. Bird beaks were used for decorations.

Horses: Spaniards brought the horse to America. At first, Indians were afraid of the horse or thought it was sacred. Later, Indians "broke" horses gently, often "hypnotizing" them with a blanket. Horses were used for trade, barter or payment. Some Indians ate horse meat in hopes of gaining the animal's power.

Hunters: Early Indiana natives may have hunted now-extinct mammoths & mastodons! When those animals disappeared, they hunted deer, elk & bison.

Huntington: City laid out in 1832 at the heart of the once-powerful Miami Nation. Here you can see the Chief Richardville House & Miami Treaty Grounds.

Indian: In 1493, Christopher Columbus called the native people he met "Indians" because he mistakenly believed he had sailed to India! Today, this term includes the aborigines of North & South America.

Indiana: Means "Land of the Indians."

Indian Awareness Center: Fulton County Historical Society, Rochester. Potawatomi & Miami Indians with roots in Indiana & others are members. Establishing a Trail of Death Regional Historic Trail with markers from Indiana to Kansas, commemorating the forced removal in 1838 of the Potawatomi.

Indian File: Walking one behind the other, the way Indians marched.

Indian Gift: When you give someone something, then ask for it back. Came from Indian custom of expecting to receive a more valuable gift than you gave. If you didn't, you demanded your original gift back!

Indian Reservations in Indiana: Indiana Miami Council, Huntington; Miami Nation, Peru; Upper Kispoko Band of the Shawnee Nation, Kokomo.

Indian Wars: Fighting in the eastern part of the U. S., prompted by fur trading, disrupted the Indians in our state & caused settled tribes to begin to move. The Miamis & their relatives, the Weas, Potawatomis, Kickapoos, & Piankashaws had just recently come to Indiana in the early 1700s. The Delawares, Munsees & Shawnees lived on the Atlantic seaboard until bloody wars drove them into our state. Everything was in such constant transition, that most Indian tribes stayed only 25-50 years in our area before moving westward.

Jacal: A house built from adobe & wood.

Jerked Meat: Thin strips of buffalo, elk, deer or other animal meat dried on racks in the sun; also called jerky.

Jesuit Father Jacques Marquette: Believed he may have landed on Indiana's shores even before early French explorers! Was just one example of the dedicated priests who braved the wild terrain to bring Christianity to the Indians.

Jesuits: Roman Catholic priests. Jesuits were among the 1st to come in contact & live with some North American Indians. Their writings, sent back to Europe, are one of the best early reference sources we have on Indian life.

Math Problem 1:
"Hard as a Brick!"

You and your family are building a jacal. You need 375 bricks of adobe. If your family can make 15 adobe bricks each day, how many days is it going to take to make enough bricks to build your jacal? Draw your jacal below.

Kickapoo: Algonquian Indian tribe that once roamed today's Wisconsin. Allied with the Sauk & Fox from early history. Some fought in the Black Hawk War of 1832.

Killed Pottery: Pottery broken during death ceremonies. It was believed that if pottery was broken, the spirit of the dead person would be released so it could travel.

Kinkash: 1832 band of Potawatomi Indians that lived on the Tippecanoe River.

Knife: Made from bone, reed, stone, wood, antler, shell, metal or beaver, bear or other animal teeth. Used in craftwork & as a weapon.

Knots: Tied on bowstrings, spearhead & arrowhead lashings, snowshoes & other items. Sometimes used to keep track of "days" like a calendar — each knot equalled 1 day.

Kokomo: Miami village named after their chief. The name means "young grandmother." Today the site of the Indiana city of the same name.

Math Problem 2: "Too Many Moons!"

You are an Indian child. Your 2 older brothers have gone on a long journey. They promised to bring you gifts when they return. Your mother has been keeping track of the days they've been gone by tying knots in a strip of buckskin, 1 knot for each day. There are 40 knots in the buckskin. You know that your brothers are going to be gone for 2 "moons," (1 Indian moon= 1 Indian month). There are 28 days in an Indian moon. How many days longer do you have to wait to get your presents?

Lance: Spear used for hunting & war. The hunting lance had a short shaft & a broad, heavy head. The war lance was light & had a long shaft.

Lariat: A throw rope made of rawhide, buffalo or horsehair. Some were up to 20 feet long!

Leggings: Cloth or skin covering for the legs; worn by both men & women. Often decorated with quillwork, beads or painted designs.

Lenápe or Leni-lenápe: What the Delaware Indians called themselves; means "real men."

Little Munsee Town: Former Indian village located near Anderson, Indiana.

Little Turtle: Miami chief. Boldest of the Indian leaders in the Northwest Territory. Born near today's Fort Wayne. Had an excellent military mind. In battle, combined tactics used by white generals with the Indians' ability to fight in the wilderness. In 1790, lured an army led by Gen. Josiah Harmar into the Maumee River Valley, which he defeated with a surprise attack. In the next year, he defeated Gen. Arthur St. Clair's army near today's Portland. With 360 of 3,000 men killed, this was the largest defeat of the U. S. Army by the American Indian. In 1797, visited Washington, D. C. Met a Polish general who gave him a pair of pistols & had his portrait painted by Gilbert Stuart, the famous artist who painted George Washington's portrait.

Logansport: Named for Shawnee chief Spemicalaba.

Love & Marriage: Many of the early French explorers & fur traders, called *voyageurs*, who came to Indiana married Indian women.

Menoquet: Potawatomi village once located in Kosciusko County.

Miami: Algonquian Indians who established the most permanent roots in Indiana. Lived here around 150 years, in central & northern Indiana. Their territory extended from the middle Wabash River to what today is the city of Fort Wayne. Formed a crucial alliance with the Shawnee. They called themselves *Twightwees*, a name that came from the cry of the crane. Worshiped the sun & thunder. Lived in cabins covered with rush mats. Were slow spoken & polite. They cut off a woman's nose if she was unfaithful to her husband. By 1827, they had sold all their lands & moved to Kansas. Lived in villages where they grew corn, beans & pumpkins. Houses were made of poles stuck in the ground covered with bark or cattail mats. Patches of deerskin carefully sewn together were their clothes. The villages were filled with music & dance during festivals. They played instruments made of drums of animals skins & rattles made of gourds. They were very religious, believing in an all-powerful creator, other lesser gods, life after death & good & evil spirits that lived in the forests, rivers & even inside of rocks!

Mississippi Culture: Constructed mounds as religious shrines. In some parts of the American Midwest, these peoples existed into the 1600s.

Mound Builders: About 2,000 years ago a wave of migrating people came to our area. They were the 1st of many groups to be known as the Mound Builders, for the earthenworks they created. Sometimes built high earthen walls around their villages, possibly for defense. They vanished long before the 1st white explorers reached Indiana.

Mounds: Great hills of earth made by human hands. Can be round with broad, flat tops, cone-shaped, or in the shape of animals. Created by early peoples of Indiana. Were used to mark graves of important community members. At least 1/3 of all the counties in Indians today contain remains of such mounds.

Mounds State Park: Near Anderson on the White River. Site of 10 ancient earthworks built by Woodland Indians more than 2,000 years ago. The largest is 360 feet around!

Names: Indian names were often changed during the person's lifetime. The names could come from things that happened during the person's birth, puberty, warfare or final retirement from active tribal life. Some names came from dreams, some were inherited & sometimes names were stolen or taken in revenge. Today, some Indians have old Indian names, while others take Christian names. Since settlers could not read or write very well, they recorded Indian names as they "sounded" & so they often were misspelled.

Neconga: Miami village once located in Indiana.

Needle: The kind of needle we think of for sewing was very rare among the Indians. They did have some needles made from bone, wood, cactus spines & the locust tree. The iron needle was brought over with the settlers. Thread used included horsehair, human hair & plant fibers.

Northwest Ordinance: With its passage, guaranteeing freedom of religion & other rights to settlers, frontier farmers stormed Indiana, which seemed like an invasion to the Indians!

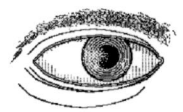

Activity: "What's in a Name?"

1. If you could pick any Indian name for yourself, what would it be?

_____

2. If you were named for something that happened in your life, what would your name be?

_____

3. What names could come from dreams that you've had? _____

Orators: Many Indian leaders were excellent public speakers. It was important that their dramatic speeches be powerful enough to influence their tribe. Watch for famous Indian quotations in literature & textbooks!

Here are some examples:

"I am the last to sign it & I will be the last to break it." — What Miami Chief Little Turtle said when he signed a peace treaty. He kept his word. When the War of 1812 started he refused to join in.

"My heart is a stone; heavy with sadness for my people, cold with the knowledge that no treaty will keep the whites out of our lands. . . . But here me: a single twig breaks, but the bundle of twigs is strong. Some day I will embrace our brother tribes & draw them into a bundle, & together we will win our country back." — Tecumseh, a Shawnee chief

Osceola, Indiana: Named after the great Seminole chief.

Ouiatenon Fort: (Say *wee-AUGHT-e-non*) One of the forts that the Indians managed to claim during the French & Indian War. Built by the French on the Wabash-Maumee water highway. From 1717-60, was a thriving fur-trading post with a population of almost 2,000.

P

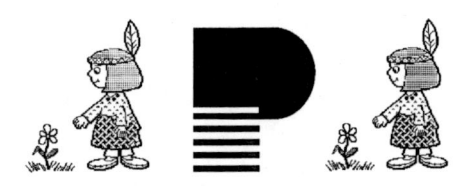

Pawnee, Indiana: Named after the powerful confederacy of Indians called the Pawnee.

Peshewah: Former Miami Indian chief. Born near Fort Wayne around 1761. Also called John B. Richardville. Became very wealthy. Russiaville (a combination of his Indian & French name) is named for him. Died in 1841.

Pokagon, Simon: Last chief of the Pokagon band of the Potawatomi Indians. His father once owned the land where Chicago stands now. Born in 1830. At the age of 14, was sent to school at Notre Dame in Indiana. Spoke many languages & was probably the most educated Indian of his day. Wrote many magazine articles & a book, printed on birch bark. Managed tribal affairs for 43 years, even helping collect a $150,000 claim from the Government. Died in 1899.

Pontiac, Chief: Brilliant Ottawa leader. In 1763, led an uprising of Great Lakes Indians against British rule. He peacefully took Fort Ouiatenon, but 2 years later, returned to the fort & ended his war in negotiation.

Potawatomi: The most advanced farmers of the Three Fires federation. Burned away grass & brush to clear fields for planting. Principal crops were corn, beans, squash & tobacco. After the harvest, they moved their villages into the forests to be protected from the winter winds.

Prophet: Brother of Shawnee chief Tecumseh. They both founded a religious community on the banks of the Tippecanoe River near today's Lafayette. When Gen. William Henry Harrison, governor of the newly-formed Indiana Territory, feared Indian rebellion, he gathered an army & marched toward the village. The Prophet told the warriors that the gods would make them invisible to the soldiers & that the bullets shot from their guns would be as soft as rainwater!

Publications from Indiana About the Indian: *Old Northwest Corporation Newsletter*, Vincennes, published by the Sonotabac Prehistoric Indian Mounds & Museum; *Museum of Heritage Newsletter*, Indianapolis; *Indian Progress*, Richmond, published by the Associated Committee of Friends on Indian Affairs; *Indian Awareness Center Newsletter*, Rochester, published by the Fulton County Historical Society; *Anthropological Linguistics Journal*, Bloomington, published by the Indiana University Department of Anthropology & the American Indian Studies Research Institute.

Quillwork: Indians used the quills of the porcupine or birds to make a type of embroidery. Quills were dyed with juice from berries & other materials. When they were ready to be used, they were mashed with the teeth or softened with hot water & flattened with rocks. The quills were laced into moccasins, shirts, pipe covers & other articles. Slowly, quillwork was replaced by beads gotten in trade with settlers.

Quirt: A short riding whip with a wood, bone or horn handle.

Quiver: Case used to hold arrows; made of cedar, otter, coyote & mountain lion skins.

Math Problem 3: "A Question of Quivers"

Some hunters in your tribe are going on a buffalo hunt. They need to bring enough arrows to kill a buffalo. Each quiver of arrows holds 20 arrows. If the hunters usually have to shoot 100 arrows to kill one buffalo, how many quivers of arrows do they need to bring?

Rain Dancing: A special dance to produce rainfall. This ceremony is common in Indian religions because the weather is so important for growing crops. The rainmakers were in tune with nature. There are many reported cases of Indians producing or preventing rain!

Rattles: Indians made rattles from bird beaks, animal hooves, bones, pods, seashells, turtle shells & other animal parts. The rattles are used in ceremonies & witchcraft.

Rawhide: Untanned hide. The green hide was stretched on the ground or over a frame. Flesh & fat were removed. The skin was dried, washed, then buried with wood ashes which made the hair come off. Used by the Indian to make drumheads, lash lodge poles, mend broken objects & in many other ways.

Read All About It!: At these Indiana Indian libraries: Archives of Traditional Music, Bloomington, recordings of Native American music & language & other oral history; Indiana University Museum Library, Bloomington, 2,000 volumes; American Indian Studies Research Institute, Bloomington; Potawatomi Museum Library, 1,000 Indian reference books; Museum of Indian Heritage Reference Library, Indianapolis, 2,000 books on Native American archaeology, art, language, plus Indian treaties, literature & more.

René -Robert Cavelier, Sieur de La Salle: 1st European explorer to visit Indiana. A Frenchman who came here in 1679. In 1681 he came to the St. Joseph River, where South Bend is today, & under the shade of a broad oak tree, met with the chiefs of the Miamis & their neighbors, the Illinois. He tried to persuade them to unite against the Iroquois, but was unsuccessful.

Russiaville, Indiana: Named for an Indian called Peshewah.

Shop Till You Drop!: At these Indiana Indian arts & crafts & cooperatives: Indian Creek Trading Post, Corydon; Skystone N' Silver, Hobart; One Earth Gallery & Gifts, Lafayette; Rainbow Art & Frame, Terre Haute; Days Past, Thorntown; American Treasures, W. Lafayette.

Slocum, Francis: White woman captured in 1779 by Indians in Pennsylvania when she was 5 years old. About 60 years lager, her relatives finally found her living with a Miami Indian husband & his tribe. She refused to return with them. Her grave & a monument are located at Mississinewa Reservoir, near Peru.

Society for Ethnomusicology: Indiana University, Bloomington; 2,000 members; study music as a part of culture.

Sonotabac Prehistoric Indian Mound & Museum, Vincennes: Largest ceremonial mound in Indiana; exhibits from 10,000 B. C. to the present.

Spemicalaba: Shawnee chief. Taken prisoner as a child by General Logan, who raised him & gave him the name of James Logan. Became a captain & fought with the Americans in the War of 1812. Died in 1812 of wounds sustained in battle.

Study the Indian!: Indiana educational institutions with Native American related programs include: Indiana University, Bloomington, American Indian Studies Research Institute; Ball State University, Muncie, Native American Studies Program; Indiana State University, Terre Haute, Indian art, cultures & many other studies; Purdue University, W. Lafayette, Indians of North America & other studies.

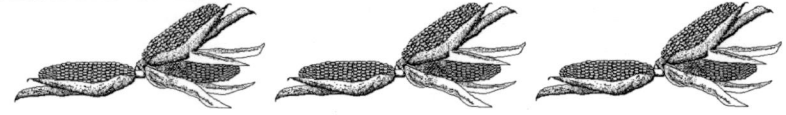

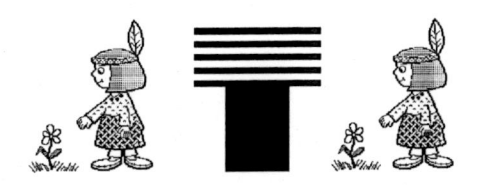

Tacumwah: Miami matriarch & mother of Chief Richardville.

Tecumseh: Shawnee leader. Passionate speaker & tireless political organizer. Persuaded the Great Lakes Indians to set aside tribal jealousies & unite against the white enemy.

Tenskwátawa: Name of Tecumseh's brother; also called "the Prophet." Fought in Indiana at the Battle of Tippecanoe.

Three Fires: The Potawatomi, Chippewa & Ottawa formed a confederation by this name. They all spoke Algonquian dialects & shared a common cultural tradition, but otherwise had different economies & day-to-day living habits.

Tippecanoe: Miami Indian name for an Indiana river. Names means "buffalo-fish place." Also the name of a village on the Wabash River which was once occupied by the Miami, then the Shawnee.

Tippecanoe Battlefield: November 7, 1811; bloody end of many Indian skirmishes. William Henry Harrison & 1,000 U. S. infantrymen marched on Prophetstown when his nemesis, Chief Tecumseh, was gone. Camping nearby, they were attacked by 600-700 Indians. After 2 hours, the Indians gave up, but many of the Americans had been killed.

Toisa: Former Potawatomi village near today's Bloomingsburg in Fulton County.

Topeah: Son-in-law of Miami chief Richardville. Also known as Francis laFontaine. Became chief & primary negotiator when the last of the Miami were relocated to Kansas in 1846.

U. S. Bureau of Indian Affairs: Provides public services to Indians.

U. S. Colonists: Were called Long Knives or Big Knives by early Indians. They called English explorers "Coat Men"!

U. S. Indian Reorganization Act: Passed by Congress in 1934 authorizing Indian tribes to establish & conduct their own governments & to form businesses.

U. S. Indian Schools: The Bureau of Indian Affairs operates 365 Federal schools around the nation, with a total enrollment of more than 43,000 Indian children.

U. S. Indian Territory: This was the former territory that is now part of the United States. It was set aside by Congress in 1829 to be used by Indians transferred from the east to the west side of the Mississippi River.

U. S. Indian Wars: The U.S. War Department came up with an official list of "Indian Wars" that occurred in the United States.

U. S. President: Once called Great White Father by Indians.

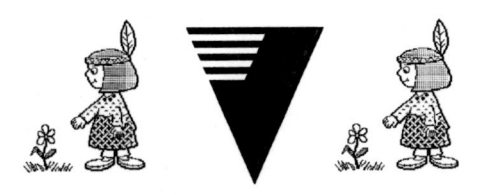

Vermillion: Kickapoo tribe that lived on the Wabash River.

Village du Puant: Former Winnebago village located in Tippecanoe County & abandoned around 1819.

Village of Mota: Potawatomi village near Atwood.

Vincennes: In 1732, became the site of the 1st Christian church in Indiana. Father Xavier de Givinne was its earliest priest. His goal was to covert Indians to Christianity.

Vesperic Indians: Indian tribes located in the United States. Here are some of the many categories of *vesperic* Indians.

Vesperic Indians Word Search

```
D E W I X K F L W G I R O Q U O I S S K
E D O W M D F L O G H J K S E O U H E W
L Z A K Y E N G H J X S P A P A G O M A
A S H W I I L N C U U A F S L N S S I H
W G S H W R D K L M O P A W N E E H N O
A D G H S J E K X U I H O P I H D O O M
R E S K D K W L C K S I N U Z S K N L H
E U D K L W O V B N X P A I U T E I E G
C T D E I R Z R T S Z A K S A T A M S F
H E S H J D A T I M U C U A S H J B S E
I K D J K S K N G E H C N A M O C G D O
N E D H A K Y D N L M C B Z C L W O V Z
O E S M L A I I I S K C M A K D O Q A A
O R S L C N J S L F J K I S K G H N E K
K C K W A K I U T L T F G H J I E R X Y
```

Categories (Words to Find)▼	Region
Chinook:	Northwest Coast
Comanche:	Midwest
Creek:	Southeast
Delaware:	Northeast
Hopi:	Southwest
Iroquois:	Northeast
Kwakiutl:	Northwest Coast
Mohawk:	Northeast
Paiute:	West Coast
Papago:	Southwest
Pawnee:	Midwest
Seminole:	Southeast
Sioux:	Midwest
Shoshoni:	West Coast
Timucua:	Southeast
Tlingit:	Northwest Coast
Ute:	West Coast
Zuni:	Southwest

Wabash: What La Salle called some Indian tribes he met in Indiana around 1682. Name means "bright," which referred to the limestone bottom of the river.

Wampum: Algonquian word for "white." This described beads or strings of beads made of clam or whelk shells. They were used in trade between the Indians & settlers. In 1640, counterfeit wampum was made!

Warpath: Meant that Indians had been agitated enough to take the only path left — battle!

War Pony: Horse, often painted with colorful paint & ridden into battle.

Wayne, Fort: Built by American General "Mad" Anthony Wayne at the confluence of the St. Marys & St. Joseph Rivers. A crude wilderness fort, it was built over the site of a former Miami Indian tribe village. The location later became one of Indiana's largest cities.

Wea: Indians located across from Fort Ouiatenon. A Miami band. Served as middlemen in the fur-trading network between the French & tribes on the prairies to the west.

West: After their defeat at the Battle of Tippecanoe, the Indians had little resistance against the whites. They were forced to flee west, leaving behind their burial mounds & the lands that had long been their home.

Wild Rice: A lakeshore crop & one of the chief foods of the Indian of the North Central states, especially the Algonquian tribes of the Great Lakes.

Wyandot: Name of the former Erie & Huron Indians that eventually located in Indiana.

...Marks the Spot!

Pick a spot in your state where you were once an Indian child. Put an X over it. Now think back to what it was like to live in that time & in that culture. What is the year? How is your lifestyle different? Use your imagination to write a diary of your typical day!

_____
_____
_____
_____
_____
_____
_____
_____
_____
_____
_____
_____

... Or, "Why?"

Questions for discussion:

1. WHY do you think Indian warriors carried charms with them? Though some of their medicines have been scientifically proven to have true healing power & are still used today, do you think their charms had any real power to help them win battles?

2. WHY do you think the American government kept relocating Indians & making the reservations smaller & smaller?

3. WHY did Indians use items like a pipe in ceremonies? What kinds of symbolic objects do we use in ceremonies today?

4. HOW did Indians use natural materials in creative ways?

5. Many Indian tribes are running successful businesses on their reservations today. There is one industry that many tribes are making a lot of money at. Do you know what this is? Hint: "I'll bet you do!"

6. WHY do some Indian tribes have a lot of problems with alcoholism and even suicide?

ZZZZZ...

Shamans & medicine men were not the only ones that had access to the spirit world. Indians believed that people could make contact with spirits every night in their dreams! Dreamers could travel back to the time of man's creation or far ahead into their own futures. They also believed that dreams contained warnings or commands from the spirits. Many tribes felt that they had to act out their dreams as soon as they awoke. If an Indian dreamed about bathing, for example, he would run to his neighbors' houses first thing in the morning & his neighbors would throw kettles full of cold water over him.

Have an Indian "daydream," & describe it in the space below:

_____

_____

_____

_____

_____

_____

_____

Zachariah Cicot: Son of a French father & Potawatomi mother. Served as a scout for American army leaders. Later founded the town of Independence.

Writing Activity:
An Indian Journey

Pretend that you are an Indian child in a small tribe. Although the shaman has performed many rain dances, there is a terrible drought. The crops are dying, & your tribe is going hungry. Your parents & other adults in the tribe decide that you must move. What will you take with you? How will you travel? What dangers might there be on the journey? What skills will you & your family use to help you in your travels?

_____

_____

_____

_____

_____

_____

_____

_____

_____

Bibliography

Cherokee Publications
P. O. Box 430-G
Cherokee, NC 28719
704-488-8856
Has a great catalog which features books, videos, cassettes, maps, kits, & other items. Our favorite item is the Map of North American Indians. Excellent tool to get your bearings on which Indians are where. Includes the U. S. & Canada.

Concise Encyclopedia of the American Indian
by Bruce Grant
Copyright 1958
Published by Wings Books, 49 Engelhard Ave., Avenel, NJ 07001
Often found on bargain tables for under $10, this book is an excellent resource for students. Over 200 drawings, pronunciations, Indian Tribe Family Tree, distribution of Indian tribes by state & selected list of museums & books.

Dictionary of the American Indian
by John Stoutenburgh, Jr.
Copyright 1960/Wings Books
Extensive A–Z listing covering U. S. & Canada.

Myths of the North American Indians
by Lewis Spence
Copyright 1994
Published by Gramercy Books, 40 Engelhard Ave., Avenel, NJ 07001
A $10 value on the bargain tables, this book features many myths & legends of North American Indian tribes. A bibliography, glossary & index are included.

North American Indian Arts
by Andrew Hunter Whiteford
A Golden Press Book
This small, inexpensive pocket guide is well-organized & indexed. It's quick & easy to use with full-color artwork throughout. Very helpful to determine one tribe's handiwork over another's.

Think Tank

❶ IF YOU WERE AN INDIAN WHO HAD LIVED OFF FISH YOU CAUGHT, HOW WOULD YOU FEEL ABOUT TODAY'S HIGH LEVELS OF WATER POLLUTION?

❷ DO YOU THINK SPORTS TEAMS SHOULD HAVE INDIAN NAMES, CHANTS, ETC.?

❸ WHY DO YOU THINK SOME TRIBES BOUND THEIR CHILDREN'S HEADS TO MAKE THEM FLAT? WHAT OTHER CULTURES DO SIMILAR THINGS? WHY? WHAT DOES *YOUR* CULTURE DO?!

❹ IS IT IMPORTANT TO PRESERVE NATIVE AMERICAN LANGUAGES, ART, CULTURE, IDEAS & HISTORY? WHY OR WHY NOT?

❺ WHY IS IT IMPORTANT FOR ORAL HISTORY OR MUSIC TO BE SHARED *ACCURATELY*?

❻ THE CHEROKEE CHIEF, SEQUOYA, BELIEVED THAT WHITE PEOPLE HAD GREAT POWER BECAUSE THEY COULD READ & WRITE. THIS IS ONE REASON HE INVENTED AN ALPHABET FOR HIS TRIBE. IS THE ABILITY TO READ & WRITE A "POWER"? HOW NECESSARY IS AN ALPHABET FOR THIS "POWER"?

Glossary

❶Assaricol or asseroni: "big knife" or "he who makes axes"; what the Iroquois called the white man

❷Bedalpago: "hairy mouths"; what the Kiowa called the white man, meaning their mustaches

❸Gooktlam: "pig tail"; what the Indians called the Chinese

❹Kentahere: what the Mohawk called Scotchmen; the word referred to the type of hats they wore, which the Indians thought looked like cow or buffalo droppings!

❺Ma'kadawiyas: "black flesh or black face"; what the Indians called people with black skin

❻Ta-'ka-i: "his ears stick out"; what the Kiowa called the white man

❼Wameqtikosiu: "builders of wooden ships"; what the Indians called the French

❽Wautacone: "coat men" or "one who wears clothes"; what the Indians called the Englishmen

❾Wayabishkiwad: "white skin"; what the Chippewa called the white man

❿Yah Yah Algeh: "those who talk ya ya"; what the Indians called the German & Dutch

Pop Quiz

1. Why did Indians break pottery during death ceremonies?

2. What did Indians do to affect the weather & help their crops?

3. What is an "adze"?

4. Who made treaties with the Indians?

5. What kind of bird is very important to Indians?

6. What is an Indian religious leader called?

7. What is the name of a sacred instrument symbolizing rain, lightning & thunder?

8. What is an Indian word for "baby"?

9. What beads made of shells were used for trade between Indians & settlers?

10. How did Indians explain thunder & lightning?

11. Where did the name "Indian" come from?

12. What is another name for Indian corn?